CONNECTICUT

CONNECTICUT

HELLO U.S.A.

by Amy Gelman

 Lerner Publications Company

You'll find this picture of a white oak at the beginning of each chapter in this book. Connecticut's official state tree is a white oak called the Charter Oak. In 1687 a colonist put Connecticut's charter in a large white oak tree to hide it from an agent of the English king. The Charter Oak fell down in a storm in 1856, but Connecticuters have honored it as their state tree since 1947.

Cover (left): Sailboats on the Connecticut River near Essex. Cover (right): Yale University, New Haven. Pages 2–3: Downtown Hartford. Page 3: Gillette Castle near Chester.

Copyright © 2002 by Lerner Publications Company

This book is available in two editions:
Library binding by Lerner Publications Company, a division of Lerner Publishing Group
Soft cover by First Avenue Editions, an imprint of Lerner Publishing Group
241 First Avenue North
Minneapolis, MN 55401 U.S.A.

Website address: www.lernerbooks.com

Library of Congress Cataloging-in-Publication Data

Gelman, Amy, 1961–
    Connecticut / by Amy Gelman — Rev. and expanded 2nd ed.
        p.   cm. — (Hello U.S.A.)
    Includes index.
    Summary: An introduction to the land, history, people, economy, and
environment of Connecticut.
    ISBN: 0–8225–4077–0 (lib. bdg. : alk paper)
    ISBN: 0–8225–0774–9 (pbk. : alk paper)
    1. Connecticut—Juvenile literature. [1. Connecticut.] I. Title. II. Series.
F94.3.G45 2002
974.6—dc21   2001006020

Manufactured in the United States of America
1 2 3 4 5 6 – JR – 07 06 05 04 03 02

CONTENTS

Rustic farms make up part of Connecticut's rural appeal.

THE LAND

Forests, Fields, and Foothills

Connecticut is a tiny state—one of the smallest in the nation. The state often surprises visitors, who wonder how such a small place can offer so many different landscapes. Scenery around the state varies from forests and rolling hills to lush farmland and sparkling beaches.

Connecticut is the southernmost state in New England, a name that refers to the northeastern corner of the United States. Rhode Island lies to Connecticut's east, and Massachusetts is its neighbor to the north. New York borders Connecticut to the west, and Long Island Sound (an inlet of the Atlantic Ocean) forms the state's southern border.

Mountain laurel, the state flower, brightens Connecticut's mountainsides.

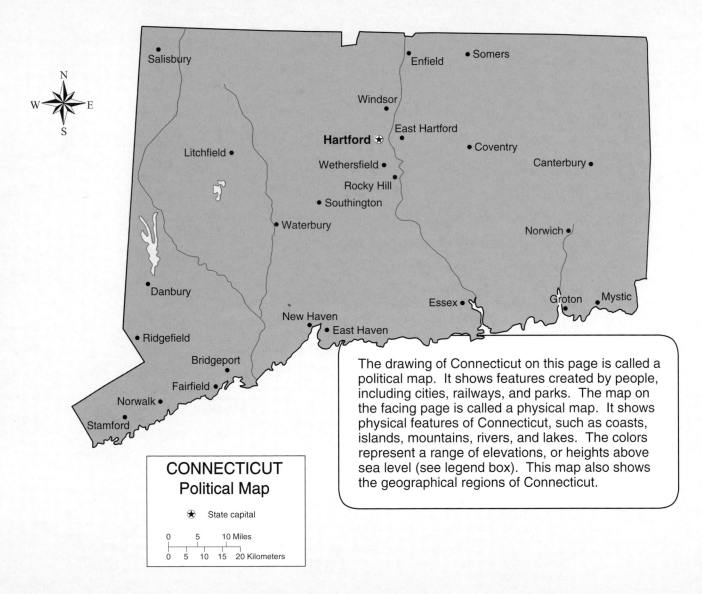

The drawing of Connecticut on this page is called a political map. It shows features created by people, including cities, railways, and parks. The map on the facing page is called a physical map. It shows physical features of Connecticut, such as coasts, islands, mountains, rivers, and lakes. The colors represent a range of elevations, or heights above sea level (see legend box). This map also shows the geographical regions of Connecticut.

CONNECTICUT
Political Map

⊛   State capital

0   5   10 Miles

0   5   10   15   20 Kilometers

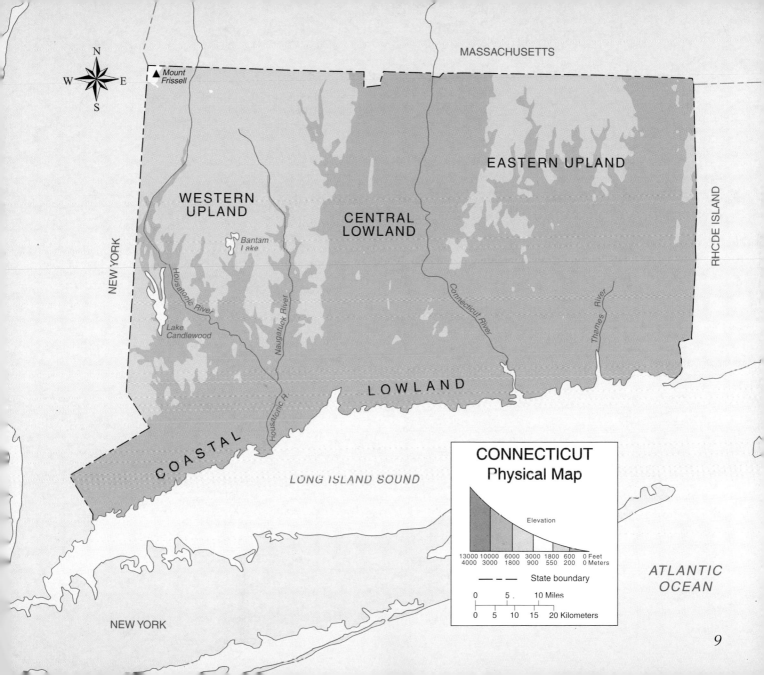

N
W · E
S

Mount Frissell ▲

MASSACHUSETTS

WESTERN UPLAND

EASTERN UPLAND

CENTRAL LOWLAND

NEW YORK

Bantam Lake

Housatonic River

Naugatuck River

Lake Candlewood

Connecticut River

Thames River

RHODE ISLAND

Housatonic R.

LOWLAND

COASTAL

LONG ISLAND SOUND

NEW YORK

ATLANTIC OCEAN

CONNECTICUT
Physical Map

Elevation

| 13000 | 10000 | 6000 | 3000 | 1800 | 600 | 0 Feet |
| 4000 | 3000 | 1800 | 900 | 550 | 200 | 0 Meters |

— — — State boundary

0   5   10 Miles

0   5   10   15   20 Kilometers

Events that happened long ago helped shape Connecticut's landscape. Over 200 million years ago, volcanic lava flowed up from inside the earth and spread over central Connecticut. The lava hardened into ridges of solid rock, which still rise out of parts of central and eastern Connecticut.

More recently, about 30,000 years ago, solid sheets of ice called **glaciers** covered what later became the northeastern United States. As these glaciers melted, they too changed Connecticut's terrain. The glaciers dragged piles of soil, rocks, and pebbles along the ground, making hills and ridges throughout the state. The melting ice filled hollow areas, creating many lakes and streams.

Most of the hills formed by the glaciers are in two regions, the Western Upland and the Eastern Upland, at either end of the state. The flatter Central Lowland region lies in between. In the southern part of the state, the narrow Coastal Lowland runs the length of Long Island Sound.

Connecticut's highest peaks tower over the Western Upland. The southern slope of Mount

Colonial buildings dot the banks of the Connecticut River, which begins at the Canadian border and flows through four states before emptying into Long Island Sound.

Frissell, the highest point in the state, rises to 2,380 feet in the northeastern corner of the region. Much of the Western Upland is still **rural,** with few big cities.

The Central Lowland, which boasts Connecticut's best farmland, covers the central part of the state. Green, fertile valleys and wide ridges of volcanic rock make up the region's landscape. The long Connecticut River flows through much of the Central Lowland. Hartford, the state capital, lies on the western side of the river.

The hills of the Eastern Upland are lower than those in the Western Upland, and dense forests cover much of the area. Gently sloping hills and broad rock ridges alternate with fields and valleys.

Connecticut's Coastal Lowland attracts many local and out-of-state vacationers.

The Coastal Lowland, lower and flatter than the rest of the state, runs along the southernmost edge of Connecticut. The region claims several of the state's largest cities. Sandy beaches cover the southern part of the Coastal Lowland. Many people who live in this region travel to nearby New York City to work.

The Connecticut is the state's major river. Many Indian tribes once made their homes on the river's banks, and early white settlers built the state's first towns there. Its name (and the state's) comes from an Indian word, *quinnihtukqut*, meaning "at the long tidal river." The Housatonic, the Naugatuck, and the Thames are other important rivers.

More than 1,000 lakes dot the Connecticut countryside. The largest of these is Lake Candlewood. An artificial lake, Candlewood was created when a

dam, or barrier, was built across the Housatonic River. Construction workers dug a hole to store the water blocked off by the dam, and this stored water became Lake Candlewood. Glaciers carved out Bantam Lake, the state's largest natural lake.

Weather in Connecticut—as any Connecticuter will tell you—can be unpredictable and often varies quite a bit from one part of the state to another. Temperatures are generally coolest in the upland hills and warmest in the lowlands. Winter temperatures in Connecticut average between 25° and 30° F. Summer temperatures usually range between 68° and 72° F.

Connecticut summers are usually comfortably warm, but the chilly winter turns Connecticut's landscape snowy.

Black-capped chickadees *(right)* inhabit Connecticut's countryside, and small mammals like the beaver *(below)* thrive in the state's lush forests and streams.

Connecticut has a lot of people for such a small state. They have crowded out most of the large animals, such as bears and panthers, which once prowled the land. Many small furry creatures, including rabbits, beavers, minks, and squirrels, still roam Connecticut's fields and forests. A few fishers, small mammals that are cousins of the weasel, can be seen there too. White-tailed deer and a few moose occasionally roam through the woods.

Forests of ash, beech, birch, and oak cover much of Connecticut. Flowering mountain laurel bushes, which decorate hills and roadsides all over the state, are a familiar sight to people traveling through Connecticut's colorful landscape.

Connecticut's many forests provide its residents and visitors with a beautiful display of fall color.

Natives and Newcomers

ong before the first Europeans arrived in Connecticut, hundreds of Native American, or American Indian, groups lived all over the area. Among them were the Niantic, the Podunk, and the Nipmuc. These people hunted animals and gathered wild plants for food in Connecticut's dense forest. They fished in its waters. Later, their descendants grew crops such as corn and tobacco.

Wigwams, made from saplings and large sheets of bark, housed many Native Americans in the Connecticut area.

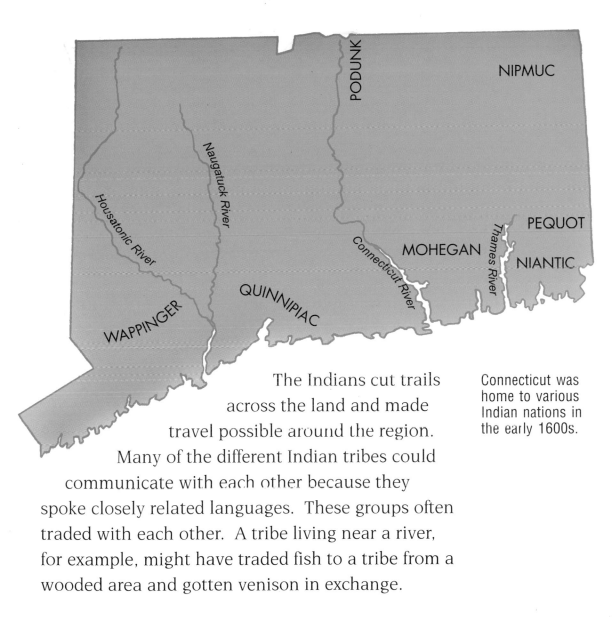

The Indians cut trails across the land and made travel possible around the region. Many of the different Indian tribes could communicate with each other because they spoke closely related languages. These groups often traded with each other. A tribe living near a river, for example, might have traded fish to a tribe from a wooded area and gotten venison in exchange.

Connecticut was home to various Indian nations in the early 1600s.

In the late 1500s, people from the Pequot nation moved into what later became Connecticut. The Pequot, whose name is said to mean "destroyers of men," quickly became the most powerful Native American group in the region. They took over control of some of the land from other tribes.

At about the same time, many Europeans were exploring North America. The first European known to have reached Connecticut was a Dutch explorer, Adriaen Block. He sailed up the Connecticut River in 1614, hoping to set up trade with the Indians.

When Block returned home, he described with enthusiasm the land he had seen. His reports led a number of people from the Netherlands to move to the Connecticut River valley. These people settled near what later became Hartford.

Their settlement became part of the Dutch **colony** of New Netherland. This large area was controlled by the government of the Netherlands, which was thousands of miles away. The colony included parts of modern-day New York, New Jersey, and Delaware, as well as part of Connecticut.

The Dutch settlers bought land from the Pequot and traded with many local Indian groups. The newcomers exchanged European goods, including guns and alcohol, for seeds, crops, lumber, and animal furs.

Establishing trade with the Indians was important to the success of the Dutch colonies.

As the Dutch were settling in, people from the nearby Massachusetts Bay Colony were also exploring the fertile Connecticut River valley. They were **Puritans**—believers in a strict form of Christianity—who had left their home in Great Britain because they were not permitted to practice their religion there. As Massachusetts Bay became too crowded, some Puritans headed south.

The newcomers settled in and around three towns (later named Windsor, Wethersfield, and Hartford) on the Connecticut River. The towns formed the colony of Connecticut. Like other British settlers in nearby colonies, the Puritans of Connecticut followed the orders of the British government.

A tour through the town of Windsor reveals Connecticut's first church.

A group of Connecticut's first Puritan settlers, led by Reverend Thomas Hooker, left the Massachusetts Bay Colony in 1638.

In 1638 more Puritans came to the region from Massachusetts Bay. They felt that the people of the Massachusetts Bay Colony weren't religious enough. They formed another colony, called New Haven, near Long Island Sound.

At first, the members of the two Puritan colonies lived in peace with their Indian neighbors. The colonists traded with local tribes, who taught the settlers to grow crops such as corn and beans.

As more European settlers came to the colonies, Native Americans willingly sold much of their land to the colonists. But the Indians believed that no one truly owned the land. They were sure that the colonists would let them keep using the land even after they had sold it.

The Europeans, however, did not share this attitude. As the settlers' demands for land increased, the Indians found they had less and less land. Where were they to hunt and grow crops? The relationship between Europeans and Indians became tense. The Pequot, who wanted more land to use, were especially unhappy with the colonists.

Violence soon broke out between the Pequot and the settlers. No one is sure which side began the fighting, but the Pequot and Puritans attacked each other several times during 1636. Finally, in 1637, Captain John Mason and his troops carried out one of the most terrible massacres of Indians in American history. Mason's forces burned the main Pequot village, killing about 600 people in all.

The once-powerful Pequot were almost completely destroyed. The smaller Indian groups that remained were unable to stop the white people from taking over Indian land.

This cemetery contains the graves of Hartford's first settlers, including Reverend Thomas Hooker.

The Puritans devised this battle plan to destroy the Pequot fort in Mystic in 1637.

Many of the Indians who remained were killed in other battles, such as King Philip's War. This war was named after the tribal leader Metacomet, called King Philip by the whites. Hundreds of other Indians died of diseases they caught from the Europeans.

By the middle of the 1600s, most of the people in the colonies of Connecticut and New Haven were white people of British origin. A few hundred black Africans had been brought to the colony of Connecticut in the early 1600s to work as slaves. The Dutch, who were outnumbered in the colonies by the British, had given up all claim to their settlements in the region.

Although white settlers were still under British rule, they wanted to set up a local government to take care of day-to-day business in the colonies. The leaders of the Connecticut Colony drafted the Fundamental Orders of 1639. Some people believe that this document influenced the writing of the U.S. Constitution. The Fundamental Orders gave people the right to elect their own governor.

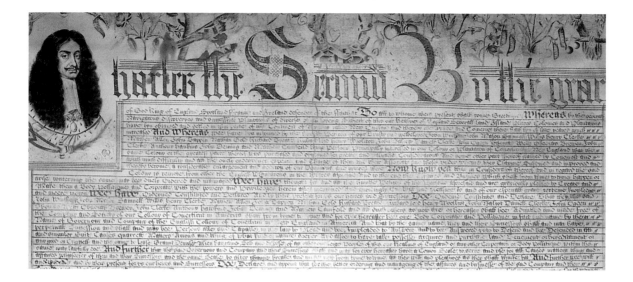

In 1662 King Charles II granted the colony of Connecticut some freedom from British rule.

In 1662 King Charles II of Britain granted Connecticut a charter, which replaced the Fundamental Orders. The charter set boundaries for the region and required that the Connecticut and New Haven colonies combine into one under the name of Connecticut.

In the mid-1700s, the British government decided to take more control of all 13 of its North American colonies. It placed high taxes on everyday items such as sugar and tea. The colonists felt that these taxes were unfair.

One of the most resented of the new taxes was the Stamp Act. This tax forced the colonists to pay for special stamps that the British government required on all newspapers, legal documents, and other printed materials.

The government of Connecticut accepted the stamp tax, but many of its citizens did not. Some of them (including Jonathan Trumbull, who later became governor of the colony) joined a group called the Sons of Liberty to oppose the new taxes.

The British government thought it could regain control of the colonies by taking back their charters. Connecticuters disagreed. They hid their charter in an old tree—the Charter Oak in Hartford. The Charter Oak (*left*) is no longer living, but a monument stands in its place, serving as a powerful patriotic reminder.

The Sons of Liberty refused to use British goods. When a high tax was placed on tea, for example, the Sons of Liberty and their followers gave up tea and drank coffee instead.

These actions, and similar protests in the other American colonies, eventually forced the British to cancel almost all of the taxes. But the colonists still resented British control and decided to break away. They prepared to fight for their independence.

At Fort Griswold, Connecticuters in costume reenact a battle from the American War of Independence.

The first battles between British and American troops broke out in Massachusetts in April 1775. More than 3,000 men from Connecticut rushed to Massachusetts to join in the fighting. The battles quickly led to full-fledged war—the American War of Independence.

Connecticuters supported the American cause in many ways. The colony's farmers provided crops and cattle for hungry American troops. Manufacturers made guns and ammunition. The colony provided so much help for the army that people began to call it the Provisions State.

In the summer of 1776, representatives from each of the 13 American colonies signed the Declaration of Independence. This document declared freedom from British rule for the 13 colonies.

The dream of independence became a reality when the British surrendered in 1782. The American War of Independence officially ended the following year, and the United States was born. In 1788 Connecticut proudly joined the new nation as its fifth state.

During the 1800s, Connecticut developed a reputation for producing quality goods. Many Connecticuters found it profitable to travel to other states selling their wares. Yankee peddlers became well known around the country.

As the 1800s began, **Yankees** (as the descendants of New England's Puritans were often called) in Connecticut gained a reputation for being clever and hardworking. At that time, many people went to work in the factories that manufacturers were building along the Connecticut and other rivers.

Water surging through dams on the state's many waterways turned huge engines that created electricity. This form of energy, called **hydropower**, was an inexpensive source of the electrical power needed to run machines at the state's factories.

Land of Steady Habits

In addition to high-quality goods, Connecticut has long been known for its many **insurance** companies. The first insurance company in the state was formed in 1795. A Hartford company sold the nation's first accident insurance, which protected a local businessman on the short walk to and from his office.

People and businesses pay insurance companies to protect them and their possessions in case of emergencies. For example, you can buy health insurance so that if you break your leg while playing sports, the insurance company will help pay your doctor's bill. Other common forms of insurance include accident and theft insurance for cars and fire insurance for homes and businesses.

Connecticut's insurance companies have a reputation for always paying what they promise. They have earned the state an unofficial nickname—the Land of Steady Habits.

Nearly 100 insurance companies have made their home in the state—about half of them in Hartford. In fact, Hartford is sometimes called the Insurance City.

Many insurance companies operate out of Connecticut, including the Travelers Insurance Company, which occupies the Travelers Tower *(above)* in Hartford.

— Colt's Firearms Company of Hartford —

The famous Colt pistol, invented in 1836, has been manufactured in Connecticut since 1855. Samuel Colt's gun-making factory in Hartford produced many high-quality guns, such as the Texas Arm (above), which was used in the Mexican-American War (1846–1848). Colt invented the first handgun that could be fired several times in a row without stopping. Colt pistols were also widely used in the Civil War (1861–1865), and by the end of the 1800s had been part of many famous shoot-outs in the American West.

In the early 1930s, an economic slump known as the Great Depression hit the United States. In Connecticut, many factories and other businesses closed. Native Connecticuters and new immigrants alike lost their jobs. Because the state's economy centered around industry, poverty was widespread during this period.

When the United States entered World War II in 1941, the people of Connecticut once again helped supply the armed forces with guns, ammunition, and soldiers. Many people who had been out of work were able to find jobs in factories that produced these goods and other items for the war effort. Connecticut's economy, along with the rest of the country's, quickly improved.

Many of the state's residents relocated to the suburbs. As transportation methods improved, New Yorkers sought housing on Connecticut's less-crowded land and commuted to work in New York City. The population's expansion to the suburbs pulled attention away from the major cities, which began to show their age.

With a high rate of migration around the state, Connecticut decided it needed a new system of electing legislators. The state adopted a new constitution in 1965. This document secured a fairer arrangement, based on the population of each district, to elect Connecticut's representatives.

Political changes in the 1980s lessened the need for the production of military materials, and many Connecticuters working in the manufacturing industry lost their jobs. They either found work in a growing service industry or sought employment in other states, and Connecticut began to prepare their students for the future of American jobs.

As this modern skyscraper reflects, Connecticut is a combination of both new and old styles.

Since the 1990s especially, Connecticuters have invested time and money in reviving their major cities. Many of the efforts center on improving schools and neighborhoods. The late 1990s also saw an influx of immigrants attracted to Connecticut's many opportunities. The majority of the state's new residents arrived from Haiti, Vietnam, and Central America.

Connecticuters are known for their hard work and inventiveness. Their state is prosperous, and its jobless rate is low. Nationally, Connecticut ranks near the top in the average amount of money its citizens earn. As they look to the future, the people of Connecticut continue their tradition of hard work and innovation.

PEOPLE & ECONOMY

The Provisions State

uch has changed in Connecticut since the first Europeans arrived. Perhaps the most noticeable change has been in the state's landscape. The countryside in which the Indians made their home hasn't disappeared, but alongside it are lively, bustling cities and suburbs. Much of the land in Connecticut is covered with forests, but homes, businesses, roads, and other signs of human activity are widespread too.

About 3.4 million people live in Connecticut. That's a huge number for such a small state. Connecticut has about 4 times as many people as Montana—even though Montana is almost 30 times larger than Connecticut.

Most people in Connecticut live in **urban** areas (cities and suburbs), but small, uncrowded towns can still be found in the countryside. In fact, people often move to Connecticut because it offers many peaceful little towns that are not too far from the convenience and excitement of big cities such as Boston and New York.

Connecticut's land includes lively cities such as Hartford *(below)* and serene countryside.

People who live in Connecticut trace their origins to many different parts of the world. This is a change from the state's Yankee days, when most residents were British or Native American. Most modern-day Connecticuters were born in the United States. Many are descended from the immigrants who came to the state during the 1800s and 1900s.

The largest racial group in Connecticut is white. Within that group, Italian Americans make up the state's largest ethnic group, followed by people of Irish and British origin. Descendants of Germans, Poles, and French people are among other large groups.

Latinos make up the second largest racial group in Connecticut. Nearly 10 percent of the state's residents are Latino. About 9 percent of Connecticuters are African American, and about 2 percent are Asian American.

About 8,000 Native Americans, including members of tribes native to Connecticut, live in the state. The state runs five Indian reservations, and less than 3 percent of Connecticut's Native American

Native Americans in Connecticut celebrate their heritage at Schemitzun—the Annual Feast of Green Corn and Dance.

population lives on them. Other Native Americans, many of whom are part Indian, live in cities and towns throughout the state.

Connecticut has long been known for high-quality education. One of the best-known colleges in the country, Yale University, is found in New Haven, Connecticut. The state can also claim the nation's first school devoted to teaching only law—Tapping Reeve Law School in Litchfield.

One of the most respected colleges in the country, Yale University, is located in New Haven.

PRUDENCE CRANDALL,
PRINCIPAL OF THE CANTERBURY, (CONN.) FEMALE
BOARDING SCHOOL.

RETURNS her most sincere thanks to those who have pat-
ronized her School, and would give information that on
the first Monday of April next, her School will be opened for
the reception of young Ladies and little Misses of color. The
branches taught are as follows:— Reading, Writing, Arithmetic,
English Grammar, Geography, History, Natural and Moral Phi-
losophy, Chemistry, Astronomy, Drawing and Painting, Music
on the Piano, together with the French language.

☞The terms, including board, washing, and tuition, are
$25 per quarter, one half paid in advance.

☞Books and Stationary will be furnished on the most rea-
sonable terms.

For information respecting the School, reference may be
made to the following gentlemen, viz.—

ARTHUR TAPPAN, Esq.
Rev. PETER WILLIAMS,
Rev. THEODORE RAYMOND
Rev. THEODORE WRIGHT, } N. YORK CITY.
Rev. SAMUEL C. CORNISH,
Rev. GEORGE BOURNE,
Rev. Mr. HAYBORN,

Mr. JAMES FORTEN, } PHILADELPHIA.
Mr. JOSEPH CASSEY,

Rev. S. J. MAY,—BROOKLYN, CT.
Rev. Mr BEMAN,—MIDDLETOWN, CT.
Rev. S. S. JOCELYN,—NEW-HAVEN, CT.
Wm. LLOYD GARRISON } BOSTON, MASS.
ARNOLD BUFFUM,
GEORGE BENSON,—PROVIDENCE, R. I.

An announcement for the opening of Prudence Crandall's school for African American girls lists the courses that Crandall offered.

Not all Connecticuters have always been able to go to school. In 1833 educator Prudence Crandall opened a school in Canterbury for black girls. Shortly after the school opened, however, angry white townspeople forced the school to close. Although most Connecticuters believed that blacks should not be slaves, not all of them wanted blacks to have the same rights as whites.

Arts and culture thrive in Connecticut, and the state boasts an unusual variety of museums. These range from the Barnum Museum in Bridgeport, which features exhibits from P. T. Barnum's famous circuses, to the renowned Peabody Museum of Natural History at Yale University.

Connecticut is an important center for regional theaters. Perhaps the best known of these is the Long Wharf Theatre, where many plays are first performed before they go on to larger audiences in New York City. Many notable writers, drawn to the state's peaceful beauty, live in Connecticut. Children's author and illustrator Maurice Sendak of Ridgefield is one of these residents.

The Barnum Museum in Bridgeport exhibits Tom Thumb's circus finery.

Fans in Connecticut cheer for sports teams from colleges such as the University of Connecticut *(right)*. A Connecticut boy fly-fishes in one of the state's many lakes and streams *(below)*.

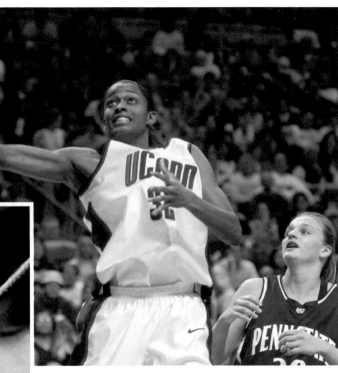

Connecticut doesn't have any professional sports teams, so fans support college teams. College teams such as the University of Connecticut's basketball team—the Connecticut Huskies—draw their share of fans.

The Pepperidge Farm plant in Norwalk produces baked treats sold around the country.

Most employed people in Connecticut (about three-fourths of the state's workers) work in service jobs helping people or businesses. Service workers include nurses, bank tellers, store clerks, and lawyers. In Connecticut, however, the best-known service is probably the insurance industry, which protects people and their property.

Manufacturing continues to be a leading industry in Connecticut, although its role in the state's economy has decreased in recent years. Nearly one-fifth of the money earned in the state comes from manufacturing, which employs about one out of seven Connecticuters.

A factory worker in East Hartford assembles a jet engine.

Instead of the hats, clocks, and ships for which Connecticut's manufacturers were once known, the state's workers now turn out modern items such as submarines, electrical and computer equipment, engines and propellers for jet airplanes, and parts for other machines. Pez candy and Lego toys are also among the goods made by Connecticuters.

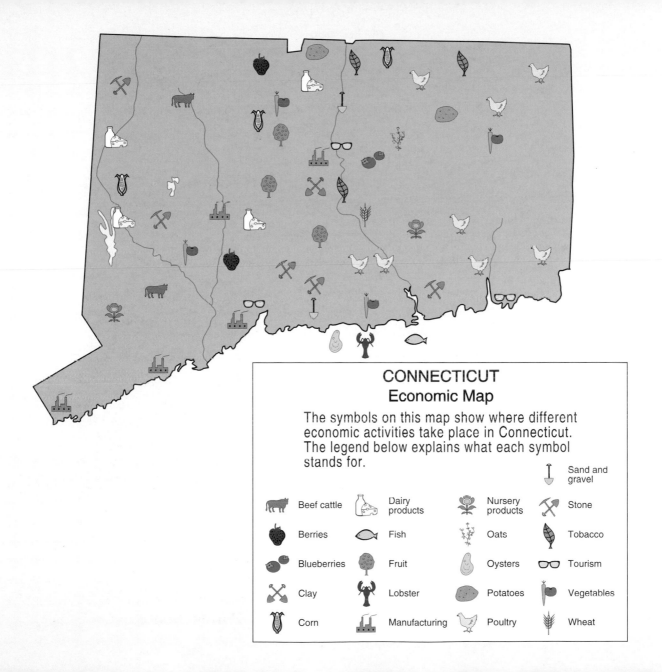

CONNECTICUT
Economic Map

The symbols on this map show where different economic activities take place in Connecticut. The legend below explains what each symbol stands for.

			Sand and gravel
Beef cattle	Dairy products	Nursery products	Stone
Berries	Fish	Oats	Tobacco
Blueberries	Fruit	Oysters	Tourism
Clay	Lobster	Potatoes	Vegetables
Corn	Manufacturing	Poultry	Wheat

Most of Connecticut's residents were farmers when the state was first settled. Agriculture became less important in the 1800s, when land became scarce and many people went to work in factories. Nonetheless, Connecticuters still run more than 3,800 farms. They produce goods such as shrubs and other plants, eggs, milk, and tobacco, which provide a small part of the state's income.

At a farmer's market in Hartford, shoppers purchase fresh local produce, like the crops of this farmer from the Connecticut River valley.

Hammonasset Beach State Park in Madison, Connecticut, offers a fun day at the beach.

Stone mined from quarries in Connecticut's Central Lowland region was used in many buildings in the 1800s and early 1900s. Crushed stone from the region is still used for paving roads and making concrete. Mining of this stone adds a small amount to the total money earned in the state.

Tourism also contributes to Connecticut's earnings. Throughout the year, tourists enjoy the activities that Connecticut offers. In the summer, some tourists sunbathe, sail, and swim on Long Island Sound. Others fish in the state's waters. In the fall, people flock to rural Connecticut to admire the changing colors of autumn leaves. Tourists spend about $5 billion in the state each year.

THE ENVIRONMENT

Conserving Connecticut's Waters

In the late 1980s, Connecticut's waterways made the news as gallons of waste leaked into Long Island Sound. Many fish and shellfish were killed, along with birds living in the marshes near the shore. Swimming was forbidden at many beaches.

This news caused great concern to many Connecticuters. Their state's numerous rivers, lakes, and streams, and Long Island Sound along its southern coast, have been important to the region since the first inhabitants arrived. The mighty Connecticut River was the site of many early settlements, both Indian and white.

Birds such as these swans in the Connecticut River *(above)* depend on clean water. Pollution from sources like garbage threatens the health of Connecticut's waters *(opposite page)*.

The abundance of water in Connecticut, along with the lack of much fertile land, helped the state's industries to develop in the 1800s. Machine shops, textile mills, and factories were built on the state's waters, where they could use hydropower as a source of energy.

Connecticut's waterways are dotted with factories such as this textile mill in Putnam.

Sewage sometimes spills into lakes and waterways.

While Connecticut's industries have helped keep the state's economy strong, they have also contributed to pollution in the state's waters. Over the years, many factories have poured chemicals and wastes into the rivers and streams of the state. These chemicals are often poisonous to the fish and other creatures that live in and near the waters.

Connecticut's large and growing human population has also added to the pollution problem. People create **sewage,** which moves with water through sinks, toilets, and other fixtures that humans use. Water that contains sewage is called **wastewater.**

Wastewater from a treatment plant has polluted these oyster beds.

Solids, oil, and some other pollutants are usually removed from wastewater at treatment plants before it is released into the state's water supply. But treated wastewater still contains some pollutants that cause damage to waterways.

Much greater damage is done if sewage leaks into waterways before it has been treated. Raw sewage makes water unsafe to drink or use for cooking or washing. Raw sewage leaks are what forced the beach closings of the late 1980s.

Rainwater that carries pollutants is also called wastewater. Rainwater brings pollutants to **storm sewers,** underground pipes that empty into Connecticut's waterways. These pollutants come from many sources, such as landfills where garbage is buried, and even from lawns and gardens, where people spread chemicals to help plants grow.

Where Wastewater Comes From

Wastewater comes from sinks, toilets, baths and showers, and even lawns and gardens. It travels through sewers and eventually ends up in waterways.

Lawn and Garden: Chemicals such as fertilizers and pesticides wash off lawns when it rains, and the rainwater carries these pollutants to the nearest storm sewer. Watering the lawn or garden too heavily can also add pollutants to wastewater.

Bathroom: Waste and water from toilets, sinks, showers, and baths add to the wastewater that goes through sewage treatment plants.

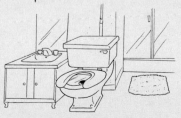

Kitchen: Kitchen cleaning products and soapy water from dishwashers and washing machines empty into drains that go to sewage treatment plants. Eventually, the wastewater enters waterways.

Car: Cars drip oil and other chemicals onto roads and driveways. These pollutants drain into storm sewers. Used motor oil poured on the

road will also end up in a nearby waterway. Even the cleaners used to wash a car add to wastewater pollution.

Connecticut's government has taken steps to make its waters cleaner. It passed a law forbidding most industries to pour chemicals directly into waterways. If companies don't obey this rule, the government makes them pay for each fish they kill in Connecticut's waters.

Volunteers clean up the area around a farm in New Britain. Connecticuters find many ways to protect their state's water resources.

Some individuals are trying to help control water pollution, too. A group of commercial fishers, for example, patrols Long Island Sound to make sure that sewage plants don't dump raw sewage into the water.

Connecticuters who are worried about their state's water can take other steps to prevent pollution. Using less water at home can help avoid leaks at sewage treatment plants, which usually occur when the plants are overloaded with sewage. Even turning off the water while brushing teeth can make a difference.

To maintain their state's beauty, these Connecticuters cooperate to remove the trash from Long Island Sound's beaches.

A ferry crosses the Connecticut River near Chester. The people of Connecticut are enjoying their state's cleaned-up waterways.

Because of the efforts of Connecticut's government and people, rivers such as the Connecticut are the cleanest they have been since the 1800s. Many rivers and streams that were once badly polluted are becoming safe again for fish and for swimmers. To

further protect Long Island Sound, Connecticut developed a conservation plan in 1995 that helps to keep cleanup efforts on track. With long-term care, Connecticut can continue to offer the beauty and variety that have drawn people to it for centuries.

Fun Facts

Connecticuters must have quite a sweet tooth. The Bradley-Smith Company in New Haven, Connecticut, made the world's first lollipop in 1908. Other candies created in the state include Mounds and Pez.

Connecticut adopted Nathan Hale as its official hero in 1985. Hale, born and raised in Coventry, Connecticut, was a spy for General George Washington in the American War of Independence. He was caught by British soldiers and hanged in 1776.

One of the best places in the world to see ancient dinosaur tracks is Dinosaur State Park in Rocky Hill, Connecticut.

The state chose Prudence Crandall as its official heroine in 1995. Crandall attempted to establish a school for African American girls in the 1800s. Her efforts met with violent opposition. Crandall is treasured as an early supporter of racial equality.

Stone mined in Connecticut has been used in many buildings around the country and even farther away. Buckingham Palace, the home of the British royal family in London, England, has a piece of Connecticut.

Connecticut is the third smallest state in the country—only Rhode Island and Delaware are smaller. Connecticut is so small, in fact, that it would fit into Alaska, the largest state, more than 117 times.

The *Hartford Courant*, first published in 1764, is the oldest U.S. newspaper in continuous publication.

Making plaster molds of footprints is a popular family activity at Dinosaur State Park.

STATE SONG

"Yankee Doodle" was a favorite battle song of American soldiers during the American War of Independence. The state of Connecticut adopted the song as its official state song in 1978.

YANKEE DOODLE

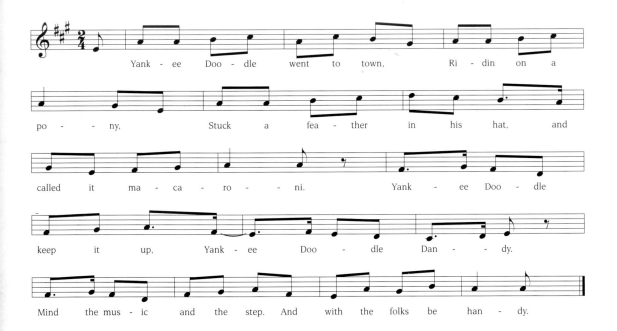

You can hear "Yankee Doodle" by visiting this website:
<http://www.state.ct.us/emblems/song.htm>

A CONNECTICUT RECIPE

Connecticut has been a pioneer in the candy industry. In 1908 the Bradley-Smith Company in New Haven, Connecticut, made the world's first lollipop. Some people say that George Smith of the Bradley-Smith Company named the hard candy on a stick after a local racehorse named Lolly Pop.

In Connecticut and around the world, lollipops come in many flavors, from cherry to chocolate. Flavors are available in the grocery store as extracts. You can find them near the spices. Lollipop molds and sticks can also be found at the grocery store or bakery. The recipe below makes 25 to 30 lollipops.

LOLLIPOPS

You will need:

1 cup sugar
½ cup light corn syrup
½ teaspoon flavoring
6 to 10 drops food coloring

½ cup confectioners sugar
lollipop molds
lollipop sticks

1. Mix sugar and light corn syrup in a small, microwave-safe bowl.
2. Cover with plastic wrap and microwave on high for 3 minutes.
3. Carefully remove plastic wrap and stir mixture.
4. Cover with new plastic wrap and microwave for another 3 minutes.
5. Remove from microwave.
6. Add flavoring and coloring. Stir well.
7. Pour candy into molds and arrange sticks.
8. Let candy cool and harden.

HISTORICAL TIMELINE

20,000 B.C. The first Indians arrive in what later became Connecticut.

late 1500s Pequot Indians move into the Connecticut area.

1614 Adriaen Block sails up the Connecticut River, becoming the first European to see what later became Connecticut.

1633 Puritans settle Windsor; Wethersfield and Hartford are settled in 1634 and 1636.

1636–1637 A war develops between the Puritan settlers and the Pequot. Puritan soldiers defeat the Pequot by burning their main village.

1662 King Charles II of Britain grants a charter, a guarantee of rights, to the colony of Connecticut.

1687 British authorities attempt to revoke some of the freedoms secured by the charter. Angry Connecticuters resist Britain's control by hiding their charter from the royal governor.

1775 Three thousand men from Connecticut join in the first battles between the British and American armies.

1788 Connecticut becomes the nation's fifth state.

1795 The first insurance company in Connecticut is formed.

1848 Connecticut outlaws slavery.

1861 Many Connecticuters join the Northern side during the Civil War.

1860s A large number of Irish immigrants arrive in Connecticut.

1900 A 10-year wave of immigration from Europe to Connecticut begins.

1930s Many businesses close in Connecticut because of hard economic times during the Great Depression.

1965 Connecticut adopts a new constitution.

1988 Connecticut celebrates 200 years of statehood.

1990s A new wave of immigrants from Haiti, Vietnam, and Central America settle in Connecticut.

1999 Connecticut is ranked top in the nation in the average amount of money its citizens make.

OUTSTANDING CONNECTICUTERS

Benedict Arnold

John Brown

Samuel Clemens

Charles Henry Dow

Benedict Arnold (1741–1801), born in Norwich, Connecticut, was a respected American military officer. In the middle of the American War of Independence, however, he joined the British forces. His name has become part of our language—to say someone is a Benedict Arnold means that person is a traitor.

John Brown (1800–1859) was a famous opponent of slavery. Before the Civil War outlawed slavery in America, Brown helped slaves escape to Canada, where they could be free. He also led a group of men to battle in Kansas to keep Kansas from allowing slavery. Brown was born in Torrington, Connecticut.

Samuel Clemens (1835–1910), better known as Mark Twain, was a great American author. Among his most popular books are *The Adventures of Tom Sawyer* and *The Adventures of Huckleberry Finn*. A native of Missouri, Twain lived in Hartford, Connecticut, from 1871 to 1891 and wrote some of his most famous books there.

Prudence Crandall (1803–1890) opened a boarding school for African American girls in Canterbury, Connecticut, despite local prejudice. She was arrested and put on trial for disobeying a state law. Although violence eventually forced Crandall to close her school, she is remembered for her work for racial equality.

Charles Henry Dow (1851–1902), born in Sterling, Connecticut, was a financier (a type of businessman). With Edward D. Jones, he founded the *Wall Street Journal*, a daily business newspaper. Dow and Jones also created the Dow-Jones average, which gives people information about the stock market.

Ella T. Grasso (1919–1981), born in Windsor Locks, Connecticut, was the first woman in the United States to be elected governor in her own right. (Earlier female governors had taken over the office from their husbands after their husbands had died.) After holding various state and national offices, Grasso became governor in 1975 and stayed in office until 1980.

Ella Grasso

Katharine Hepburn (born 1907) has had a long and successful career as an actress. She has won four Academy Awards for her acting—more than anyone in the history of movies. Hepburn was born in Hartford, Connecticut.

Katharine Hepburn

Charles Ives (1874–1954), a great American composer, was born in Danbury, Connecticut. He graduated from Yale University and became a successful executive in the insurance company he founded. Ives, who influenced many with his innovative musical style, composed in his spare time. He won the 1947 Pulitzer Prize for his *Symphony No. 3.*

Charles Ives

Aaron Bunsen Lerner (born 1920) is a professor emeritus of the Yale University School of Medicine. He is well known for his skin research and for the many doctors he has trained. Lerner lives in Woodbridge, Connecticut.

Joe Lieberman (born 1942), a senator since 1988, graduated from Yale College and Yale Law School. He ran as the vice presidential candidate with Al Gore in the 2000 presidential race. Lieberman, born in Stamford, resides in New Haven, Connecticut.

Aaron Lerner

J. P. Morgan

Ralph Nader

Paul Newman

Adam Clayton Powell Jr.

John Pierpont (J. P.) Morgan (1837–1913) was a financier. He founded the U.S. Steel Corporation, the first company in the world to be worth $1 billion. He was born in Hartford, Connecticut.

Ralph Nader (born 1934), from Winsted, Connecticut, is well known for his efforts to protect people from products that are unsafe. Since the 1960s, he has been calling attention to problems with certain cars, chemicals, and other goods to make people aware of the possible dangers of using these products. He ran in the 1996 and 2000 presidential races on the Green Party ticket.

Paul Newman (born 1925) has been a popular movie actor for many years. He studied acting at the Yale Drama School in New Haven, Connecticut, and has lived in Westport, Connecticut, since the early 1960s. He also owns a food company, Newman's Own, that donates all of its profits to charity.

Frederick Law Olmsted (1822–1903), a landscape architect, was born in Hartford, Connecticut. Olmsted's designs include Central Park in New York City and the grounds of the U.S. Capitol. In addition to urban development and park design for big cities around the country, he also helped to establish Yosemite as a national park.

Adam Clayton Powell Jr. (1908–1972) was a member of the U.S. Congress from 1944 to 1970. For much of his career, he was one of only two blacks in Congress. He was also a pastor of the Baptist church. Although he lived in New York for most of his life, Powell was born in New Haven, Connecticut.

Maurice Sendak (born 1928) is an author and illustrator of children's books. He started his career as a comic-book artist. Perhaps his best-loved book is *Where the Wild Things Are*. Sendak lives in Ridgefield, Connecticut.

Harriet Beecher Stowe (1811–1896) was born in Litchfield, Connecticut. An abolitionist and author, Stowe wrote many anti-slavery pieces. Her most renowned work, *Uncle Tom's Cabin*, was published in 1852. The novel helped increase awareness of the cruelties of slavery.

Harriet Beecher Stowe

Bonnie Tiburzi (born 1950) is from Danbury, Connecticut. In 1973, she became the first woman to be hired as a pilot by a major airline.

Bonnie Tiburzi

Uncas (1588?–1683?), born a Pequot Indian of Connecticut, led some of his people to form a new tribe called the Mohegans. The Mohegans fought on the side of the British colonists during the Pequot War. After the Pequots were defeated, Uncas became the leader of the surviving Pequots.

Noah Webster (1758–1843) was a lexicographer (a person who makes dictionaries). He was also a lawyer, teacher, and journalist. Webster, born in West Hartford, Connecticut, began publishing dictionaries in 1806. Revised versions of *Webster's Dictionary* are still widely used.

Noah Webster

Eli Whitney (1765–1825) of New Haven, Connecticut, invented a system of manufacturing interchangeable parts that was put to use all over the world. The method made it possible to put goods together much more quickly than they could be made by hand. Whitney's other inventions include the cotton gin, a machine that pulls fibers off of cotton seeds.

Eli Whitney

FACTS-AT-A-GLANCE

Nickname: Constitution State

Song: "Yankee Doodle"

Motto: *Qui Transtulit Sustinet* (He Who Transplanted Still Sustains)

Flower: mountain laurel

Tree: white oak

Bird: American robin

Hero: Nathan Hale

Heroine: Prudence Crandall

Insect: praying mantis

Mammal: sperm whale

Mineral: garnet

Date and ranking of statehood: January 9, 1788, the fifth state

Capital: Hartford

Area: 4,845 square miles

Rank in area, nationwide: 48th

Average January temperature: 26° F

Average July temperature: 71° F

Connecticut adopted its state flag in 1897. The vines on the white shield represent the first European settlements. Below the shield, a white ribbon bears the state motto.

POPULATION GROWTH

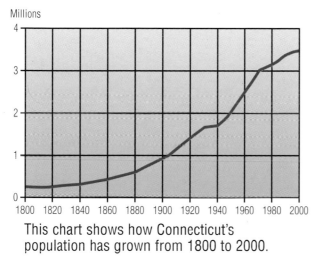

Millions

This chart shows how Connecticut's population has grown from 1800 to 2000.

As on the state flag, three vines and the state motto adorn the state seal. Connecticut adopted the seal in 1784.

Population: 3,405,565 (2000 census)

Rank in population, nationwide: 29th

Major cities and populations: (2000 census) Bridgeport (139,529), New Haven (123,626), Hartford (121,578), Stamford (117,083), Waterbury (107,271)

U.S. senators: 2

U.S. representatives: 5

Electoral votes: 7

Natural resources: clay, gravel, sand, soil, stone, water

Agricultural products: eggs, greenhouse and nursery products, milk, tobacco

Mining products: crushed stone, gravel, sand

Manufactured goods: chemicals, fabricated metal products, food products, machinery, primary metals, printed materials, rubber and plastic products, transportation equipment (including jet engines and submarines)

WHERE CONNECTICUTERS WORK

Services—68 percent (services includes jobs in trade; community, social, and personal services; finance, insurance, and real estate; transportation, communication, and utilities)

Manufacturing—14 percent

Government—11 percent

Construction—5 percent

Agriculture—2 percent

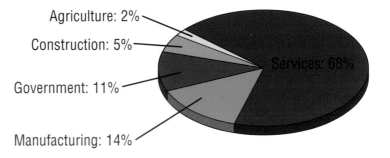

Agriculture: 2%
Construction: 5%
Government: 11%
Manufacturing: 14%
Services: 68%

GROSS STATE PRODUCT

Services—70 percent

Manufacturing—17 percent

Government—9 percent

Construction—3 percent

Agriculture—1 percent

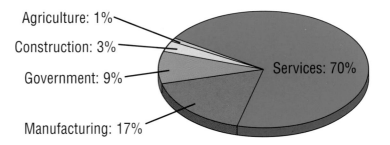

Agriculture: 1%
Construction: 3%
Government: 9%
Manufacturing: 17%
Services: 70%

STATE WILDLIFE

Mammals: black bear, flying squirrel, muskrat, striped skunk, white-tailed deer

Birds: eastern bluebird, gray-cheeked thrush, house wren, Nashville warbler, northern cardinal

Amphibians and Reptiles: eastern spadefoot toad, green frog, northern water snake, small brown snake

Fish: American eel, Atlantic salmon, gizzard shad, pickerel, shortnose sturgeon, striped bass

Trees: American chestnut, fire cherry, hackberry, redbud, sour gum

Wild plants: butterfly weed, climbing bittersweet, ostrich fern, trumpet honeysuckle, wild geranium

A birdhouse makes a cozy home for an Eastern bluebird and its hungry offspring.

PLACES TO VISIT

Dinosaur State Park, Rocky Hill

This park allows visitors to examine one of the largest dinosaur track sites in North America. A geodome contains over 500 uncovered Jurassic fossil tracks nearly 200 million years old. Visitors can make a mold of a dinosaur footprint.

Essex Steam Train, Essex Junction

Passengers ride in cars pulled by an old-fashioned steam locomotive on this 12-mile tour of the Connecticut River Valley.

Indian Burial Grounds, Norwich

A sacred Mohegan burial ground still stands on this site. This final resting place holds a monument to Uncas, the Mohegan chief who presented European settlers with the land that became Norwich.

Mark Twain House, Hartford

The author lived in this house during the late 1800s. Twain modeled part of the exterior to resemble a riverboat. Visitors can also tour the house of Twain's neighbor, author Harriet Beecher Stowe, who lived across the lawn.

Mystic Marine Life Aquarium, Mystic

This aquarium features more than 3,500 specimens of marine life. Dolphins, whales, sea lions, and penguins participate in indoor and outdoor exhibits.

Mystic Seaport, Mystic

This preserved whaling village from the 1800s reminds tourists of Connecticut's maritime heritage. Several impressive historic ships still float in Mystic's harbor.

Peabody Museum of Natural History at Yale University, New Haven

This museum displays shrunken heads, meteorites, and fossils of dinosaurs and prehistoric mammals. *The Age of Reptiles*, a 110-foot mural, presents a probable landscape of the earth during dinosaur times.

Mystic Seaport

Barnum Museum, Bridgeport

This museum celebrates the life and legacy of the famed circus showman, as well as circus culture. Many items, such as Tom Thumb's clothes and props, are on display.

U.S.S. *Nautilus* Memorial, Groton

This memorial allows visitors to climb aboard the world's first nuclear submarine, which once traveled under arctic ice to reach the North Pole. Visitors can explore the sonar, torpedo, and navigation and control rooms, as well as the living quarters of the crew and captain. The nearby museum offers exhibits about the history and technology of submarines.

ANNUAL EVENTS

U.S. Eastern Ski Jumping Championships, Salisbury—*February*

Garlic Festival, Fairfield—*May*

Lobsterfest, Mystic—*May*

Pizza Fest, New Haven—*July*

Riverfest, Hartford—*July*

Outdoor Arts Festival, Mystic—*August*

Pilot Pen Tennis Championships, New Haven—*August*

Italian Festival, Enfield—*August*

Oyster Festival, Norwalk—*September*

Four Town Fair, Somers—*September*

Apple Harvest Festival, Southington—*October*

Festival of Light, Hartford—*November–January*

LEARN MORE ABOUT CONNECTICUT

BOOKS

General

Fradin, Dennis Brindell, and Judith Bloom Fradin. *Connecticut.* Chicago: Children's Press, 1997.

McNair, Sylvia. *Connecticut.* Danbury, CT: Children's Press, 1999. For older readers.

Thompson, Kathleen. *Connecticut.* Austin, TX: Raintree/Steck-Vaughn, 1996.

Special Interest

DePaola, Tomie. *26 Fairmount Avenue.* New York: Putnam Publishing Group, 1999. This autobiographical story follows the author during his family's move when he was five years old, giving an account of life in Connecticut in the late 1930s.

Lucas, Eileen. *Prudence Crandall.* Minneapolis, MN: Carolrhoda Books, Inc., 2002. This biography tells the story of Prudence Crandall, who started a school for black girls in Connecticut in the 1800s.

Murphy, Jim. *A Young Patriot: The American Revolution as Experienced by One Boy.* New York: Clarion Books, 1996. In 1776 Joseph Plum Martin joined the army at the age of 15. Murphy's text details life within the army based on Martin's personal journals.

Fiction

Avi. *Windcatcher.* New York: Simon & Schuster, 1991. While visiting his grandmother, Tony searches for hidden treasure off the coast of Connecticut.

Collier, Christopher, and James Lincoln Collier. *My Brother Sam is Dead.* New York: Simon and Schuster, 1984. For older readers. This Newbery Honor book is set in Connecticut during the American War of Independence. Tim's family is divided when his brother Sam goes off to fight for the colonies' freedom while, at home, his father supports the British.

Curtis, Alicia Turner. *A Little Maid of Old Connecticut.* Bedford, MA: Applewood Books, 1997. Ellie has many adventures when she visits her grandmother in Connecticut during the American War of Independence.

Van Leeuwen, Jean. *Hannah of Fairfield.* New York: Dial Books, 1999. A young girl, Hannah, and her family tend to their farm and the domestic chores of colonial life in Connecticut as the American War of Independence nears.

WEBSITES

ConneCT
<http://www.state.ct.us>
The official website of Connecticut's state government provides a welcome from the governor, a kids' page, and government and tourist information.

Connecticut Tourism Home Page
<http://www.ctbound.org>
Places to stay, trip ideas, and information for kids are offered on this tourism site.

Hartford Courant
<http://www.ctnow.com>
Read the news of Connecticut on this site, produced by the oldest continuously running newspaper in the United States.

PRONUNCIATION GUIDE

Block, Adriaen (BLAHK, AY-dree-uhn)

Connecticut (kuh-NEHD-uh-kuht)

Frissell, Mount (frih-ZELL, MOWNT)

Housatonic (hoo-suh-TAHN-ihk)

Massachusetts (mass-uh-CHOO-suhts)

Naugatuck (NAW-guh-tuhk)

Niantic (ny-AN-tihk)

Pequot (PEE-kwaht)

Podunk (POH-duhnk)

Thames (THAYMZ)

Wappinger (WAH-pihn-jur)

Sheep graze at sunset in the Connecticut countryside.

GLOSSARY

colony: a territory ruled by a country some distance away

dam: a barrier built to control the flow of water in a river, or a body of water held back by a barrier

glacier: a large body of ice and snow that moves slowly over land

hydropower: electricity produced by using waterpower, also called hydro-electric power

immigrant: a person who moves into a foreign country and settles there

insurance: the protection of people or their possessions against damage or loss

Puritan: a member of an English religious group that followed a strict form of Christianity. Many Puritans left Great Britain during the 1600s because they were not allowed to practice their religion there.

rural: having to do with the country-side or farming

sewage: wastewater that travels through pipes from buildings, usually to treatment plants

storm sewer: an underground pipe that carries rainwater and other materials to waterways

urban: having to do with cities and large towns

wastewater: water that carries waste, or sewage, from homes, businesses, and industries

Yankee: a resident of New England, especially someone descended from the area's Puritan settlers

INDEX

PHOTO ACKNOWLEDGMENTS

Cover photographs by © Phil Schermeister/CORBIS (left) and © Robert Holmes/CORBIS (right); PresentationMaps.com, pp. 1, 8, 9, 47; © Phil Schermeister/CORBIS, pp. 2–3, 3, 39, 51, 58–59; © Karlene Schwartz, pp. 4, 7 (inset), 16 (inset), 38 (inset), 50 (inset); © Betty Groskin/JeffGreenberg@juno.com, p. 6; Monica V. Brown, Photographic Artist, p. 7; Connecticut Valley Tourism Commission, p. 11; © Thomas P. Benincas, Jr., pp. 12, 13, 36, 41; Paul Fusco, Connecticut DEP Wildlife Division, pp. 14 (top), 50; © John D. Cunningham/Visuals Unlimited, p. 14 (bottom); © W. Cody/CORBIS, p. 15; Greater Hartford Convention and Visitors Bureau, pp. 16, 23, 48; Tim Seeley, pp. 17, 55, 63, 71 (top), 72; © Bettmann/CORBIS, pp. 19, 67 (second from bottom), 69 (second from bottom); Elizabeth Bray Wilkins, p. 20; Library of Congress, pp. 21, 24, 30, 34 (top right), 66 (second from top), 68 (top and bottom), 69 (top and bottom); State Archives, Connecticut State Library, Picture Group 220, Box 3 (photo by Gus Johnson), p. 26; © Burnstein Collection/Corbis, p. 27; Southeastern Connecticut Tourism Division, p. 28; The Travelers, p. 31; Connecticut Historical Society, p. 33 (detail); The Elizabeth Hart Jarvis Collection, p. 34 (bottom left); AP/Wide World Photos, pp. 40, 56; Prudence Crandall Museum, Canterbury, Connecticut, administered by the Connecticut Historical Commission, p. 42; The Barnum Museum, p. 43; © Reuters NewMedia Inc./CORBIS, p. 44 (top); Farmington Valley/West Hartford Visitors Bureau, p. 44 (bottom); Pepperidge Farm, p. 45; Pratt and Whitney, p. 46; © John Muldoon, Connecticut Office of Tourism, pp. 49, 80; © James Marshall/CORBIS, p. 52; John Dommers, Connecticut Coastal Program Staff, p. 53; Runk/Schoenberger from Grant Heilman, p. 54; Schooner Inc., p. 57; © 1991 Sallie G. Sprague, p. 61; Independent Picture Service, pp. 66 (top), 67 (top and bottom); The Nevada Historical Society, p. 66 (second from bottom); Dow Jones & Company, p. 66 (bottom); Hollywood Book & Poster Co., pp. 67 (second from top), 68 (second from bottom); © AFP/CORBIS, p. 68 (second from top); American Airlines, p. 69 (second from top); © Gary W. Carter/CORBIS, p. 73; © Robert Holmes/CORBIS, p. 75.